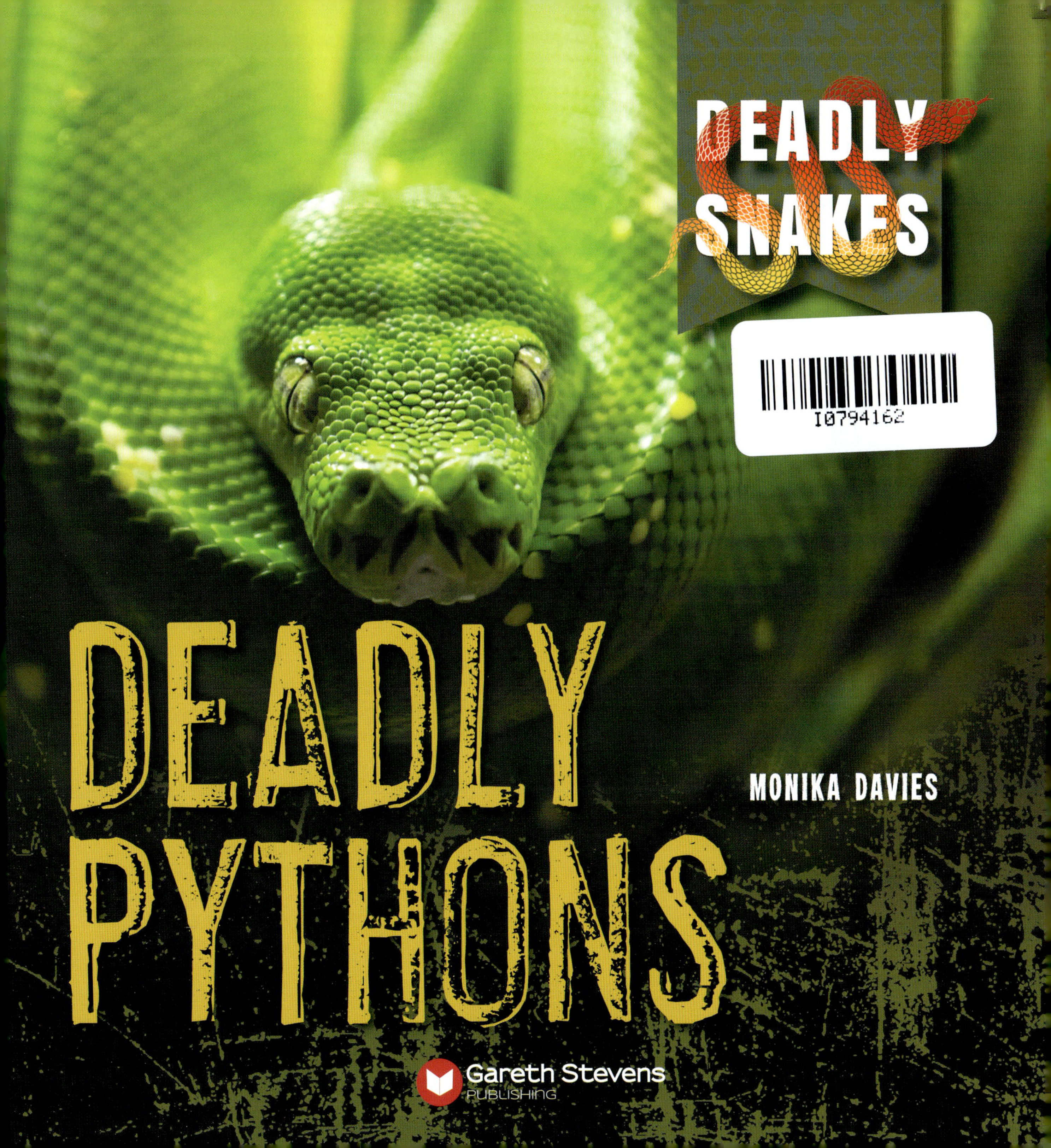

Deadly Snakes

Deadly Pythons

Monika Davies

Gareth Stevens Publishing

Please visit our website, www.garethstevens.com. For a free color catalog of all our high-quality books, call toll free 1-800-542-2595 or fax 1-877-542-2596.

Library of Congress Cataloging-in-Publication Data
Names: Davies, Monika, author.
Title: Deadly pythons / Monika Davies.
Description: New York : Gareth Stevens Publishing, [2023] | Series: Deadly snakes | Includes index.
Identifiers: LCCN 2021050753 (print) | LCCN 2021050754 (ebook) | ISBN 9781538279809 (set) | ISBN 9781538279816 (library binding) | ISBN 9781538279793 (paperback) | ISBN 9781538279823 (ebook)
Subjects: LCSH: Pythons–Juvenile literature. | Poisonous snakes–Juvenile literature.
Classification: LCC QL666.O67 D38 2023 (print) | LCC QL666.O67 (ebook) | DDC 597.96/78–dc23/eng/20211201
LC record available at https://lccn.loc.gov/2021050753
LC ebook record available at https://lccn.loc.gov/2021050754

First Edition

Portions of this work were originally authored by Amy Austen and published as *Pythons.*
All new material this edition authored by Monika Davies.

Published in 2023 by
Gareth Stevens Publishing
29 E. 21st Street
New York, NY 10010

Designer: Sheryl Kober
Editor: Monika Davies

Photo credits: Cover, p. 1 Mark_Kostich/Shutterstock.com; cover (snake illustration) vinap/Shutterstock.com; cover, pp. 1–24 (background texture) Anna Timoshenko/Shutterstock.com; pp. 1–24 (snakeskin) Natalliya85/Shutterstock.com; pp. 1–24 (halftone texture) MPFphotography/Shutterstock.com; pp. 3, 8, 19 (snake illustration) vinap/Shutterstock.com; pp. 4, 7, 11, 12, 16, 20 (fatal facts texture) Pakhnyushchy/Shutterstock.com; pp. 5, 6 dwi putra stock/Shutterstock.com; pp. 9, 21 Heiko Kiera/Shutterstock.com; p. 10 Peter Hermes Furian/Shutterstock.com; p. 13 RAYphotographer/Shutterstock.com; p. 14 Kuznetsov Alexey/Shutterstock.com; p. 15 Nynke van Holten/Shutterstock.com; p. 17 mamboo/Shutterstock.com; p. 18 Kurit afshen/Shutterstock.com;

Printed in the United States of America

CPSIA compliance information: Batch #CSGS23: For further information contact Gareth Stevens, New York, New York, at 1-800-542-2595.

CONTENTS

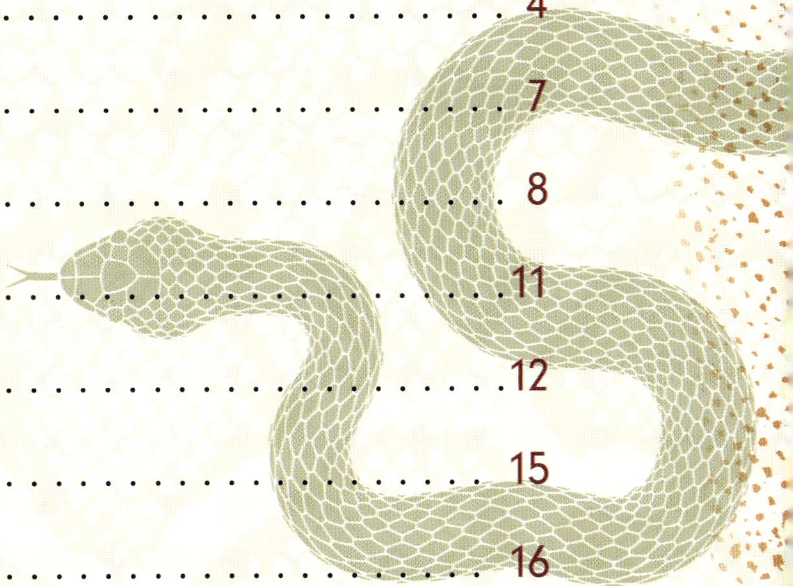

Words in the glossary appear in **bold** type the first time they are used in the text.

THE PETRIFYING PYTHON

In a forest in Southeast Asia, a giant snake waits for its next meal. Using heat-sensing "pits" on its face, the snake senses a nearby mouse. With a quick snap, the snake darts forward, sinking its teeth into the mouse. The snake wraps its body around the mouse, making it hard for the small **mammal** to breathe. Then, the snake swallows the mouse whole!

Meet the python, one of the longest—and deadliest—snakes in the world. Many animals don't want to cross paths with this snake!

FATAL FACTS

The reticulated python is known for being the world's longest snake! The Amethystine python, Burmese python, and African rock python are also three of the longest snakes.

There are around 40 different species of pythons around the world.

Pythons are known as constrictors because they use their body to constrict, or squeeze, their prey to death.

HOW TO SPY A PYTHON

Pythons come in a wide range of colors. These lengthy snakes can be brown, tan, yellowish-grey, or even bright green. You can **identify** many pythons by their long bodies. Some species can grow up to about 31.5 feet (9.6 m) long! Burmese pythons can grow to around 23 feet (7 m) and weigh up to 200 pounds (91 kg).

Pythons have sharp, curved teeth. However, pythons are not **venemonous** snakes, and they don't kill their **prey** by delivering a bite.

FATAL FACTS

Some pythons have patterns on their skin that help them blend in with their surroundings. This is known as camouflage and makes the pythons hard to spy in a thick forest.

BABY PYTHONS

Pythons hunt and eat alone. That makes them solitary animals. However, males and females come together to mate, or make babies. Some python species can lay up to 100 eggs at a time!

Most python mothers stay with their eggs until they hatch, or break open. Mothers curl around their pile of eggs. When it's cold, the mother "shivers," or makes small muscle movements. This keeps her eggs warm. When the eggs hatch, the mother leaves the nest, and her babies start their lives.

Like many newborn snakes, baby pythons must take care of themselves—without their parents' help—once they hatch from their eggs.

WHERE RETICULATED PYTHONS LIVE

The reticulated python lives across southeastern Asia. This species is found in parts of Vietnam, Bangladesh, the Philippines, and many other places.

PYTHON PROPERTY

Pythons live in many parts of the world. They are found in areas of Africa, Asia, and Australia. You can also spy them in India and China.

Pythons are found in many types of **habitats**. Some live in the rain forest, while others live on flat grasslands. Still others live in the woods or in swamps. Younger, smaller pythons hang out in trees. Bigger pythons mostly stay on the ground. Pythons are even at home in the water! Like many snakes, they're great swimmers.

FATAL FACTS

Over the years, some people have taken pythons out of their natural habitats. They brought pythons to the United States and Europe to sell as pets.

SNEAKY SENSES

Pythons are skilled hunters with **sneaky** senses. Although these snakes are not known for having the best eyesight, they have other senses to make up for it!

Each python has a special body part on the roof of its mouth called a Jacobson's organ. The python flicks its forked tongue out and collects a smell. Then, the tongue sends the smell to the Jacobson's organ, which identifies the smell. Pythons can also sense heat around them, which helps them find **prey**.

FATAL FACTS

Snakes don't have ears! Instead, they feel for vibrations, or small, quick movements, to know if prey or a predator is nearby.

Pythons often have pit organs, or small, heat-sensing holes, on their face that help them pick up heat changes around them. This is how they can “see” their prey in the dark!

A python is a slow moving predator. These snakes can only move about 1 mile (1.6 km) per hour in an open area.

FEW ENEMIES

Pythons have very few enemies because of their great **defenses**. The greatest defense for larger pythons is their size. Few predators want to attack one of the world's longest snakes! Another defense is the python's strength. If an enemy attacks, the python can give it a deadly squeeze.

Small pythons have fewer defenses. They are sometimes caught by crocodiles, large birds, large mammals, and some frogs. If an animal is larger than a python, it might try to eat the smaller snake.

WHAT'S ON THE MENU?

Pythons are far from picky eaters. They'll eat nearly anything that can fit in their mouth! They eat birds, reptiles, and mammals.

The larger the snake, the larger its prey. Pythons hunt small animals, such as rats, and big animals, such as pigs and deer. They can even swallow a crocodile! Pythons can fit large animals in their mouth by stretching their **jaws**. You can sometimes see the outline of a large animal inside a python's body!

FATAL FACTS

Pythons like to stay somewhere warm while digesting their food, or while their bodies break down the food to use it. They also need to stay still. This digestion period can take days or weeks!

There have been reports of pythons eating animals as large as deer! But most of the time, pythons are content to eat small animals, like mice.

Like many snakes, pythons don't chase their prey. They wait and strike suddenly instead.

ON THE HUNT

Pythons are **patient** hunters. They lie in wait for their prey—and then they strike, surprising their next meal! They're good at hiding from prey because their skin can blend into their surroundings. Pythons that hunt in water might hide their bodies underwater while keeping just their eyes above the surface to watch for prey.

Pythons strike quickly. They grab their prey and wind around it. Then, the python squeezes the animal tightly. This cuts off the animal's blood supply to kill it quickly.

PYTHON PROTECTION

Pythons are viewed very differently around the world. In Florida, people are trying to reduce the python population. These snakes are a big concern as they're taking over certain natural areas.

But in Southeast Asia, many are working to protect the python. Here, large parts of forests have been cut down, destroying the python's home. Pythons are also hunted for their skin. Some python species are listed as vulnerable, or open to harm.

FATAL FACTS

Pythons have become an **invasive species** in the Florida Everglades. Since pythons hunt nearly all mammals, this harms populations of Everglades animals such as racoons and bobcats. Several native species have died out because of the deadly python.

In 1992, a large and powerful storm destroyed a snake facility near Everglades National Park. Hundreds of pythons ended up escaping into the park.

GLOSSARY

defense: a way of guarding against an enemy

facility: something built for a purpose

habitat: the natural place where an animal or plant lives

identify: to find out the name or features of something

invasive species: one kind of living thing likely to spread and be harmful when placed in a new area

jaws: the bones that hold the teeth and make up the mouth

mammal: a warm-blooded animal that has a backbone and hair, breathes air, and feeds milk to its young

patient: able to wait a long time

prey: an animal that is hunted by other animals for food

sneaky: doing something in a quiet and unfair way

species: a group of plants or animals that are all of the same kind

venomous: able to produce a liquid called venom that is harmful to other animals

FOR MORE INFORMATION

Books

Boutland, Craig. *The Reticulated Python.* Minneapolis, MN: Bearport Publishing Company, 2021.

Hirschmann, Kris. *Deadliest Snakes.* San Diego, CA: ReferencePoint Press, 2017

Websites

Burmese Python

kids.nationalgeographic.com/animals/reptiles/facts/burmese-python

Discover more about the Burmese python at this website.

Python

kids.sandiegozoowildlifealliance.org/animals/python

Find out more fun facts about the python here.

Publisher's note to educators and parents: Our editors have carefully reviewed these websites to ensure that they are suitable for students. Many websites change frequently, however, and we cannot guarantee that a site's future contents will continue to meet our high standards of quality and educational value. Be advised that students should be closely supervised whenever they access the internet.

INDEX